OWN YOUR STORY

Dr. Pooja Darda   Dr. Priyanka Kokatnur

INDIA · SINGAPORE · MALAYSIA

ISBN 979-8-88883-995-9

This book has been published with all efforts taken to make the material error-free after the consent of the author. However, the author and the publisher do not assume and hereby disclaim any liability to any party for any loss, damage, or disruption caused by errors or omissions, whether such errors or omissions result from negligence, accident, or any other cause.

While every effort has been made to avoid any mistake or omission, this publication is being sold on the condition and understanding that neither the author nor the publishers or printers would be liable in any manner to any person by reason of any mistake or omission in this publication or for any action taken or omitted to be taken or advice rendered or accepted on the basis of this work. For any defect in printing or binding the publishers will be liable only to replace the defective copy by another copy of this work then available.

CONTENTS

#BUILDYOURSELF

Build your story...!!!

INTRODUCTION OF PERSONAL BRANDING

When you brand yourself, you are creating the emotional response you want people to have when they hear your name, see you on the internet, or meet you in person. Being the "correct" kind does not imply that you are someone you are not. It's everything about you that you want people to know about you: your personality, your voice, your interests, your habits, and everything else. Therefore, the information you provide to others, the things you say, and the photographs you upload should all be consistent with the theme of your individual brand. Stand-up comics are known for being "funny." Posting your jokes, links to videos of your routine, and even a link to your blog might help show others that you can be amusing. Using an online portfolio, such as a blog, is a great way for you to show off your creative abilities to the world.

THE EVOLUTION OF PERSONAL BRANDING

Everyone, regardless of their age, rank, or the industry they work in, must recognize the importance of Personal Branding. Despite the term's widespread use, there are various misunderstandings concerning the primary goal of a personal brand. When it comes to personal branding, it's not about boasting about yourself or oversharing on social media. It's more about who you are as a person and what you believe in, as well as how you show yourself to the world. Ideally, it should describe your story and reflect your vision for your life as well as your company's future.

Personal branding is sometimes misunderstood as a recent phenomenon or a catchy buzzword, so let's look at its origins first. Napoleon Hills' 1937 book Think and Grow Rich was the first to propose the concept of personal branding.

Al Ries and Jack Trout's 1981 book Positioning: The Battle of Your Mind introduced personal branding for the second time. The focus of this book is on how to position yourself to advance in your career. Individuals began to hear about personal branding in 1997 when Tom Peter wrote an article titled "The Brand Called You."

Defining a personal brand is impossible without going through an in-depth self-assessment process, which is why the three steps are mutually reinforcing and complementary. Because of this, personal branding isn't confined to social media activity. It's all about having a well-defined personal plan that reflects our deepest aspirations, passions, and beliefs, as well as the conviction we have in this vision and the steps we take to make it a reality. There are some among you who may be asking why personal branding is necessary. You all know that today we live in a very competitive, electronically moving world that is always evolving. Personal branding allows you to showcase your originality and skill; it also gives you license to be yourself and leave a mark. You need personal branding whether you're a student, a manager at a company, an entrepreneur, or a consultant to build great relationships and trust. People will only work with you if they trust you. You also need a personal brand to be able to exchange information and receive constructive feedback to retain and cultivate these connections. Just be yourself, genuine, and current if you want your Branding to succeed. A great Brand is created by being true to oneself, real, and current. If you're serious about personal branding, you'll have to put in a lot of time and work overtime, depending on how much effort you're willing to put into it.

Branding yourself will help you identify your distinctive value proposition and put it into action in the world. To make judgments that are in line with your core values, you need to use your brand as a filter. Your individuality is conveyed to the people who need to know about you through this method. To put it another way creating a personal brand is all about telling your narrative via the use of words.

However, the widespread use of social media has led to a shift in the way people think about personal branding. Modern-day social media users take use of the virtually limitless opportunities that social networking sites like Facebook and Twitter provide to openly express their thoughts and abilities. As a result of social media, personal branding is no more a privilege reserved for a select few, such as CEOs and celebrities who enjoy a lavish lifestyle. As a result, personal branding aims to ensure that every individual is given the opportunity to be heard by those who can either support them or not. These days, people use social media to broadcast their interests. Individuals create online personas based on their interests and activities, which they share with others. In the past, we needed to connect with our classmates, colleagues, and other acquaintances. The new trend is to share content with anyone who likes what we enjoy around the world.

There is no secret formula for building a strong brand, but a well-executed plan is required to succeed. According to Arruda (2009), to create a unique and appealing brand for a broad audience, consumers must go through the "extract, express, and exude" three-stage process. Identifying one's unique value proposition, expressing one's ideas and beliefs, and using the best technical tools to display the message are all part of the three-stage process.

To begin, we must discover what makes us special. What is the one thing that our audience would gain from following us on Instagram or YouTube? Next, we'll focus on developing the most effective means of communicating our ideas once we've determined their significance. To be able to openly share our opinions, we need to improve our communication abilities. Choosing the right channel is an important last step. There are countless examples of people successfully building their personal brands all over the internet. In personal branding, there is no one-size-fits-all answer.

It's also important for personal brands to communicate their message clearly, consistently, and steadfastly. Personal branding requires a high degree of clarity since it is necessary to be clear and honest about who you are and what you're not. Understand how your unique value proposition can help you gain the support of those who can help you accomplish your goals.

We are like well-known brands. We want our friends, followers, and connections to be able to find and enjoy our material no matter where or when it is published.

We transform into social entertainers, with social media serving as our stage. We believe that our posts have an impact on the people who read them. We want to gratify them and include them more fully in our activities. For example, online gamers who wish to share their enthusiasm with others desire to do it through social media. Another group of people choose to unbox the latest iPhone or to give their thoughts on a new item. Social media users must demonstrate that they are authentic and deserving of being followed on a constant basis. They solicit acceptance using likes, views, and thumbs-up signs. Welcome to the age of social entertainment on the internet.

WHY IS PERSONAL BRANDING IMPORTANT?

In today's world, personal branding has evolved into a critical approach for professionals. Online users were able to establish stronger brands through the rise of social networking websites such as Facebook and YouTube, which allowed them to showcase their abilities and passions.

Individuals in the workforce must now implement personal branding as a core strategy. This growth in the popularity of social networking sites like Facebook and YouTube has helped people build better brands to showcase their talents and interests online. An increasingly vital skill for workers in an increasingly social media-dominated economic world is the capacity to sell themselves effectively in cyberspace, To put it another way, an online brand is a resume with personality traits. In today's job market, having a strong personal brand can provide a significant competitive edge. When it comes to obtaining a solid job, the competition is fiercer than ever, and the opportunities to stand out from the throng are few and far between. There are an excessive number of candidates with university degrees and other types of qualifications.

The competitive advantage that formal education used to provide does not appear to be as strong as it once was.

Nowadays, businesses are on the lookout for natural-born leaders and skills who can propel the company forward. The pool of candidates is not restricted to a certain geographical area. Any candidate from any part of the world can search for and apply for available positions on the internet. Academic scholars look at the finest practices of personal branding in order to better understand the techniques and methods people use to improve in their professional lives. In today's international business environment, the desire to stand out from the crowd indicates personal leadership capabilities.

It is possible that one's internet image and reputation will set one apart from other job seekers. People strive for personal and professional success, and the notion that "if you don't brand yourself, others will" appears to be an inconvenient truth in this context. In the absence of a Personal Branding online account, it appears that recruiters will suspect that you are concealing something.

Personal branding encompasses more than just a YouTube channel or a LinkedIn profile. YouTube channels and LinkedIn profiles are simply part of what constitutes personal branding.

Everything you can find on the internet that is connected to your name.

The power of social media for personal branding cannot be overstated. Too much personal information is being shared online. The primary goal is to keep up with their social networks and stay in touch with their friends. Any information they post online becomes part of their digital footprint, which can be seen by everyone. If a recruiter were looking for a new employee, they would have access to any and every information that might be used to their advantage or disadvantage.

As a society, we should not overlook the importance of personal branding, which is not only a fad. A person's knowledge of how brands are formed could help them in their career. People should be aware of the positive and negative aspects, as well as the potential and risks, of their company's brand name and reputation. During a job interview, we want to show the interviewer our best selves. Personal branding encompasses more than just a YouTube channel or a LinkedIn profile.

It is anything and anything that can be found on the internet that has anything to do with your name.

Social media is a very effective technique for building one's personal brand. Users are eager to provide far too much personal information about themselves on the internet. They want to speak with their friends and stay up with what is going on in their social circles, and this is their primary goal. Nonetheless, any news, photographs, and comments they post online become part of their digital footprint, which is visible to anybody. A recruiter searching for a possible applicant may utilize any information that was accessible to him or her, either to help or hurt the candidate.

Personal branding is not a passing trend, and we should not ignore it. Someone's professional success could be aided by understanding how brands are created. People should be aware of the advantages, disadvantages, possibilities, and threats that their brand name may face. During a job interview, we strive to impress the recruiter by expressing ourselves to the best of our abilities. So, why aren't we doing the same thing when we post personal information about ourselves on the internet as well? Personal branding can be defined as how we are perceived by our target audience.

- **It assists you in determining your "Why."**

    To do what you do; you must have a clear understanding of why you're doing it in the first place. It's also what sets you apart from the other seven billion people around the world.

    The first step in developing your personal brand is to identify the values that are at the heart of who you are as a person. Some examples of core values include dependability, honesty, creativity, optimism, and service to others.

    Second, identify your passions - what are the activities that you most like doing in both your personal and professional life? These two processes will assist you in determining where you want to focus your efforts and the direction you want to go.

- ***Excellent tool for networking***

When you begin to establish your personal brand, you will begin to form relationships with other people who share your beliefs or who work in comparable fields to yours. This is an excellent method of establishing relationships and forming partnerships since you are already exhibiting who you are and what you do, making it easier to locate people who will naturally resonate with your image. Developing relationships can aid in the advancement of your profession or the natural promotion of any items or services that you provide.

- ***It establishes your authority.***

Credibility and trust are built over time because of developing your own brand. People prefer to connect with other people rather than with a faceless, nameless brand. It informs others of your identity and the reasons why they should put their trust in you. When you share content that educates your audience or establishes your expertise in a certain field, you can increase your credibility. You're establishing evidence that you're a reliable source that people can rely on.

- ***Boost Your Self-Belief***

The more time and effort you put into developing your personal brand, the more self-assurance you will get. By showcasing your individuality, you will have a better understanding of your talents and ideals. This instils confidence in you, which will aid you in furthering your professional goals or starting a new company venture.

- ***Assembles an Audience***

Building an audience is important since it may aid in the promotion of your brand, the promotion of yourself, and the connection of other people. People will follow you because they are interested in what you have to say and how you present yourself. Because they can pick and support your activities, your audience can have a significant impact on your business. You can immediately market your own business while also establishing a human connection between what you do and who you are as an individual.

- ***It helps you achieve your goals.***

Building a powerful and authentic personal brand will help you land more job interviews, move up the corporate ladder, and gain more business clients.

When it comes to business, making a good first impression is critical in today's competitive environment. Whether you meet someone in person or online, you have only seven seconds to make a good impression.

In an interview, a business meeting, or even on a first date, there is absolutely no room for error in terms of making an impression. Having a personal brand can help you make the most of any opportunity that comes your way by highlighting your skills and all the great things you have to offer.

The advantages of having a personal brand are limitless. A strong personal brand can have a favorable impact on the opportunities that are available to you in your personal life, company, and professional life. Start today, if you haven't already, to build your personal brand. Start working on your image now, whether it's updating your LinkedIn profile or starting an Instagram account.

CREATING YOUR PERSONAL BRAND: 7 STEPS TO GETTING STARTED TODAY

In today's world, branding isn't just for celebrities and Fortune 500 corporations. Making a strong personal brand is critical whether you want to advance in your career, gain industry reputation, or attract new clients. For those who doubt they have a personal brand, Google yourself.

It's a choice between letting it take on a life of its own and maintaining editorial control. To succeed professionally, you need to control your message and how the public perceives you. To build a strong personal brand, you need follow the seven steps listed above.

1-Design your brand's vision statement

It is what you believe in that is reflected in your brand vision. It's the message you'll be delivering to your audience on a consistent basis. The tone of your voice and the ideals that you hold should be communicated through your internet posts. What you stand for is encapsulated in your brand's motto. It's the message you'll be delivering to your audience on a consistent basis. The tone of your voice and the ideals that you hold should be communicated through your internet posts.

Your vision should be a concise statement that summarizes who you are, what you do, and what you stand for. While this is not something that needs to be repeated on a regular basis across your chosen social media sites, it should be kept in the back of your mind whenever you publish a post or prepare an article. When you have a well-written brand vision, it can assist you in consciously moving from where you are to where you want to be.

2-Decide on a brand name that reflects who you are

If you became known as the world's best expert on a certain subject, what would that be? Make a list of the competitors in that market and figure out how you'll stand apart. What distinguishes you from others? The only way to build a strong personal brand is to establish yourself as an expert in a specific field. Determine how you'll stand out from the competitors in that market by doing your homework on the competition. What distinguishes you from the crowd? You will be more likely to stand out from the crowd if you make use of your unique abilities. Your personal brand should accurately reflect your interests, abilities, values, and beliefs.

3-Identify Your Target Audience

The platform you use to build your online brand will change depending on your sector and your target audience. Consider the following examples: if you work in finance, LinkedIn may be the best platform for you, but if you work in the creative field, Tumblr may be the best choice for you. Choose carefully and don't overdo it—it can be tough to maintain a high level of control over many profiles. If you have personal social media accounts, make sure that the privacy settings on those accounts are kept as private as possible.

4-Develop a Single, Clear Message for Your Brand

What message do you want to reaffirm repeatedly in your content and marketing? You should use the same message throughout all your communication channels after you've decided on it. When you are consistent, you develop trust and confidence with your customers or clients. Consider using the same logo or other design components throughout all your communications. One of the keys to building a strong personal brand is to find your own unique voice and stick with it.

5-Be True to Yourself

Determine what distinguishes you from others. Then learn to embrace your individuality and utilize it to your advantage to attract people's attention and encourage them to seek out your material over that of others. People want to communicate with other people, and this necessitates being authentic. Most people want to interact with other people and being genuine is essential to that interaction. Determine what you want the personality of your brand to be. Is it more casual or more formal? Is it more fun to be silly or more serious? You will have a greater chance of having your message resonate with your audience if you make your personal brand as authentic as possible.

6-Build Your Own Website

It is necessary to have a place to display your own brand now that you have built it. You will need to create your own blog or website as a result of this requirement. With the use of pictures and material, you can demonstrate your knowledge and personality to the world. The "about me" part of your website can include a short bio and a picture of yourself. As previously indicated, you can establish distinct pages for your portfolio. You have the option of showcasing customer testimonials on your homepage or a separate page.

A consistent website or blog theme is essential to establishing and maintaining a strong personal brand. This is to ensure that you can develop your brand in the minds of your consumers, not just through words but also through pictures.

7-Make the Most of Your Online Presence

Your social media platforms, just like your website or blog, are excellent platforms for you to create and grow your own brand. There's a considerable probability that anyone who's thinking about working with or for you will do some research on you online first. And they'll very certainly look at your social media presence and behavior.

Consequently, it is critical that you optimize and maintain consistency across all of your social media sites. On each site, it will also assist you in gaining visibility among those who are conducting searches for persons with your experience or hobbies. This can be a fantastic way to network and broaden your horizons.

Use a few keywords from the bio you wrote before to optimize your social media profiles. Being that social network bios are limited in word length, you'll want to make them as clear and simple as possible while still maintaining their originality.

Begin to Build Your Network

After you've put all these elements in place, you may begin to build relationships with your peers to achieve more visibility in your field. It is possible to network by commenting on their blog entries with queries and expressions of appreciation. It could mean sharing their blog entries on social media and tagging them to express your appreciation for what they've done.

You might also follow them on social media and leave useful comments on their postings, such as opinions and queries that are pertinent to the content. At some point, you may be able to garner enough power to begin posting to their blogs and connecting with their respective fan bases. Aside from online networking opportunities, you can also meet people in person at local events and business conferences.

Create a personal brand for yourself

Name

What are your short term and long-term goal

5 Words that define your personality

5 words to define the type of career you'd like to pursue

Three abilities that you are very proud of

What do you want your surroundings to do to make you feel?

PRACTICE WORKSHEET

#THEREALYOU

Recognizing Your Strengths and Weaknesses…!!!

A SWOT (strengths, weaknesses, opportunities, and threats) analysis is a common method in the business world for evaluating a company's past, present, and future positions. It gives organizational executives with a fresh perspective on what the organization does well, where its issues lie, and which options to pursue.

If you are pursuing your professional ambitions, a personal SWOT analysis can help you achieve the same. It helps you get perspective on your strengths and limitations as a person, as well as the obstacles you'll face and the chances that are available to you now and in the future.

In the 1960s, business legends Edmund P. Learned, C. Roland Christensen, Kenneth Andrews, and William D. Guth developed the SWOT analysis as a business tool. A 2 x 2 matrix was constructed in 1982 by Heinz Weihrich to plot the answers to the four essential questions for comparison. The top row had strengths and weaknesses, while the bottom row included opportunities and threats. This is still the most popular and most efficient method of doing the investigation.

Opportunities and strengths are things you can control, whereas weaknesses and threats are out of your control and imposed by the outside world.

You can use this information to investigate the relationship between your strengths and weaknesses, how to harness your strengths to make the most of your opportunities, and how to address your weakness to reduce your threat.

WHY YOU SHOULD CONDUCT YOUR OWN SWOT ANALYSIS

When it comes to personal growth, SWOT analysis can help people become the best version of themselves. Take the time to consider what you hope to gain from your personal SWOT analysis. Do you want a new job, or do you want to make a fresh mark in your existing position by achieving more success? You might be looking for personal improvement, or perhaps you'd like to try something completely different.

Using questions regarding each of the four evaluated categories, you can conduct your own analysis. Integrity is essential for producing relevant results from an analysis.

What makes SWOT analysis so effective is that, with a little thought, it may help you uncover chances that you would not have otherwise discovered. Furthermore, by recognizing your limitations, you can control and eliminate threats that would otherwise jeopardize your capacity to move forward.

When you examine yourself through the lens of the SWOT framework, you can begin to distinguish yourself from your peers and further develop the specialized talents and abilities that will help you improve your profession and achieve your personal goals.

A SWOT analysis is a framework for identifying and analyzing your strengths and weaknesses, as well as the opportunities and dangers that you face. This allows you to concentrate on your talents, minimize your limitations, and make the most of the possibilities that are presented to you.

This assists you in thinking through the things that are essential to you and in setting compelling personal goals that will push you to achieve achievement.

WHEN TO UNDERTAKE A SWOT ANALYSIS?

Considering that it is a self-evaluation, any time is appropriate. However, there are a few cases in which it can be extremely beneficial.

1-When going to an interview - During an interview, you should concentrate on your strengths and speak about them in greater detail. As a bonus, it will assist you in preparing a CV. Additionally, if you have a very clear understanding of the job criteria ahead of time, you may tailor your CV to meet those requirements as needed. Recall that recruiters spend an average of 6 seconds deciding whether you are a good fit for their organization.

2-When seeking for a promotion - The ability to compare oneself to other candidates is beneficial while seeking for promotions. You'll have a clear grasp of your comparative advantages over your competitors, allowing you to concentrate on those advantages rather than on your overall advantages in the marketplace.

3-Before changing careers - This assessment helps you determine whether your abilities are a good match for the chances in your new career or whether they are better suited to your existing position.

HOW TO DO A PERSONAL SWOT ANALYSIS

To identify their strengths, weaknesses, opportunities, and threats, businesses frequently do a SWOT analysis. After evaluating all aspects of a situation, you can apply the same strategy to yourself when you want to make an informed decision about your next step. Being able to do a SWOT analysis may be beneficial to you as you deal with various decisions throughout your professional life.

To develop a basic SWOT analysis, start by drawing a box and dividing it into four squares. Each square represents one of the four SWOT topics: the situation's strengths, weaknesses, opportunities, and threats. Make your lists under the various categories using the squares provided. There is no limit to the number of elements you can include in the squares to build a comprehensive conclusion. Create a complete self SWOT analysis for a variety of professional scenarios by following the stages outlined below:

INTERNAL FACTORS

STRENGTHS

Don't be shy about focusing on all the positive aspects of your personality in this section. Some of the things you might wish to concentrate on are as follows:

List all of your abilities and personality traits that have helped you succeed in your life thus far and analyze them all. Possibly, you will notice some similarities

It's possible that your personal and professional lives will begin to intersect more frequently! This is significant since your soft skills are also very important in the workplace and are something that you will surely want to use if you want to develop in your profession and be promoted to a higher position.

In other words, after examining your abilities, what talents do you believe set you apart from your competitors? What sets you apart?

If you find yourself feeling uneasy at first, remember to stay positive! Every successful brand has its own USP, or Unique Selling Point, which distinguishes it from the competition. You will undoubtedly discover yours!

This will also be extremely beneficial during interviews! When asked what value you can bring to a team or what distinguishes you as an outstanding candidate, you want to be able to provide tales from your own experience.

Start with a list of all your best qualities

As a starting point, consider which aspects of your personality contribute to your success. These include any applicable qualifications, skills, and talents that you possess. Additionally, you can include formal schooling, relevant professional experiences, certificates, official recognitions, and any valuable training you have received. SWOT analysis while looking for a job can include testimonials and recommendations as well as professional connections and a readiness to relocate or work from home.

When writing a cover letter or CV for a job application, listing your strengths will help you find the most relevant qualifications. If you're preparing for an interview, you may want to mention some examples of when you used these skills and how they benefited you in that situation.

- What distinguishes you from others (skills, qualifications, education, connections)?

- What personal resources do you have?

- What do you do better than others?

- What do others regard as your strengths (especially your boss)?

- What are your proudest achievements?

- What values do you hold that others lack?

- Do you belong to a unique network? If so, who do you know?

Consider this from your own perspective and from the perspective of those around you. And don't be modest or shy; instead, be as objective as possible. To be more successful at work, it is important to identify and use your skills.

WEAKNESSES

People are sometimes uncomfortable with this part, but understanding your flaws or "areas for progress," as I like to refer to them, is critical! Learning from your mistakes allows you to identify areas of your life where you may make significant improvements and become a better version of yourself. In fact, it may even assist you in recognizing the ways in which you have already done so!

You'll be a long way ahead of your peers who haven't done this kind of deep work to figure out what they like and don't like. – It's OK to be proud of your "weak spots." They are important parts of the whole picture that is YOU!

Understand your "weaknesses"

The second stage is to identify your own personal shortcomings. As previously said, SWOT analysis is utilized by individuals to evaluate and improve their own situations. The most effective strategy to improve weaknesses is to recognize them.

You'll be more equipped to deal with them at an interview or performance evaluation if you've practiced your responses to them beforehand. Complete this by asking yourself these questions.

- Do you have the skills and qualifications required to be successful in your current or future roles?

- Do you have a poor routine? For instance, tardiness, poor communication, inaccurate time reporting, etc.

- You'll be more equipped to deal with them at an interview or performance evaluation if you've practiced your responses to them beforehand. Complete this by asking yourself these questions.

- Do you have the skills and qualifications required to be successful in your current or future roles?

- Do you have a poor routine? For instance, tardiness, poor communication, inaccurate time reporting, etc.

- Be truthful and practical in your answers to queries. Since it's a self-report only you can see, it's a good idea. Take it as a starting point for future work.

- Which responsibilities do you put off because you lack confidence in them?

- What are your perceived flaws by those who are close to you?

- Are you confident in your education and training? If this isn't the case, where do you feel most vulnerable?

    As a manager, what are some of your unfavorable work habits (for example, are you frequently late or unorganized; do you have a short temper or are you unable to handle stress)?

- Are there aspects of your personality that prevent you from succeeding in your field? For example, a fear of public speaking would be a severe drawback if you have to hold meetings on a regular basis.

It's important to look at things from both a personal and a public standpoint. Are there flaws in your character that you're not aware of? How often do your coworkers outperform you in important areas? Remain grounded; it's preferable to confront any unwelcome facts right away.

EXTERNAL FACTORS

OPPORTUNITIES

"We often miss opportunities because they are dressed in overalls and appear to be hard work" - Thomas A. Edison.

Opportunities come in many kinds and sizes. You may miss out on great possibilities because you're too busy focusing on other things. So, here are a few things to keep an eye out for.

You must be on the lookout for opportunities, and if you don't, you'll likely lose out on something worthwhile. Opportunities are everything outside of your control that has the potential to improve your current circumstances. Resources and industry trends that can help you on your career path are among these factors. If you are looking for a promotion, a new job, or an entirely new career path, you should focus on the external elements that can help you get there.

There may be substantial developments and advancements in your field that you might benefit from.

What are the current trends that you can take advantage of?

What are your long-term plans?

What are the options accessible to you?

What's the deal with improvement?

What are your options for enhancing your skills, expanding your knowledge, and enhancing your abilities?

There is no end to the questions that could be asked. Always keep an eye open for new possibilities as they arise.

It's a major plus if a job opportunity fits your skills and experience. However, tremendous chances can exist in fields where your expertise is lacking. Think about the advantages and disadvantages before you decide.

THREAT

It's external things and situations that you're concerned about, or that you fear may happen and hinder you from either accomplishing your goals or reaping the advantages of your efforts. What are the hurdles that are preventing you from attaining your goals and dreams? People, organization's, policies, situations, or even yourself could be the source of these dangers. Here are some questions to get you thinking about the dangers you face in your day-to-day life:

What difficulties are you now experiencing at work?

Are any of your coworkers in a position of competition with you for projects or positions?

Has the nature of your job (or the demand for the services you provide) changed?

Is your position being threatened by evolving technology?

Is it possible that any of your shortcomings could become a threat?

Are you being held back by someone in your life?

Ask yourself if someone in your life serves to accentuate or encourage your flaws.

Has your lack of participation in new trends, technology, and processes held you back from progressing?

If so, what are the tasks, errands, or projects that are keeping you from moving forward?

What is getting in the way of you growing in one of the other areas of your life?

Your own personal flaws could be an obstacle to your success if you don't address them.

Imagine things that, if they were different, would assist you achieve your objectives. Describe them.

Worksheet to Practice-SWOT ANALYSIS

SWOT Analysis	
Strengths	**Weaknesses**
What is it that you excel at? What distinctive resources do you have at your disposal? What do others consider to be your greatest assets?	What do you think you could do better? What areas of your life do you have fewer resources than other people? What are the most likely flaws that other will notice?
Opportunities	**Threats**
What opportunities do you have in front of you? What trends could you be able to take advantage of? What strategies can you use to transform your strengths into opportunities?	How could you be endangered? What dangers could you face? Do you know what the rest of your competitors are up to? Are you exposed to any threats because of your weaknesses?

#POSITIONINGYOURSELF

Personal Brand Statement for Creative Inspiration…!!!

Getting a job and starting a business are more difficult now than they've ever been. An effective personal branding plan is essential to your success.

Creating a powerful personal branding statement is one of the first steps in building a strong personal brand. Your brand's identity will be built around this statement, therefore it's critical to get it properly.

What is a Personal Brand Statement?

A personal branding statement is a brief description of who you are as a professional in one or two sentences. What you stand for at work can be summed up in one sentence that only you can come up with. One of the most important aspects of personal branding is the development of a personal brand statement.

Not your job title or a list of all your accomplishments, a successful brand statement is a compelling approach to market yourself in a world where human capital is becoming increasingly valuable. Finding the proper statement, on the other hand, is difficult. It needs to be concise while still reflecting the value you bring to your employers, clients, or consumers, among other things. A certain level of interest should also be there, making people want to discover more about you.

It's important to take your time and come up with something that you're fully satisfied with as your personal brand statement. Employers, clients, and consumers will appreciate your worth if your cover letter is succinct while also articulating that value. It should also be intriguing enough to make people want to know more about you.

The first thing people will remember about you is your personal brand statement, so make sure it's something you're proud of. Personal brand statements are entirely dependent on the individual and his or her personality, however the examples provided below may be helpful.

Imagine you're a digital marketer who wants to grow your business. Here's an example of what you could use for your personal brand statement:

"When it comes to digital marketing, I create effective tactics that assist firms attract more customers."

You could say something like this if you're a real estate agent:

"I can assist you in finding the home of your dreams at the price you choose. Choose your words carefully since a successful personal brand statement is brief and to-the-point. Make use of phrases that elicit an emotional response, and zero down on the one benefit you offer that people will find the most compelling."

STEPS IN WRITING A BRAND STATEMENT

1-Be Authentic

One of the primary objectives of developing a branding statement is to demonstrate who you are. People want to know who they're dealing with in the professional environment. The primary means through which you can reach this societal norm is through your own brand, which implies that your branding statement must be genuine. It's fine to tailor your message to reflect your desired persona, but always remember to be genuine to yourself. Begin by brainstorming some ideas and scribbling down words and phrases that have special meaning to you.

2-Identify your target market

Your initial branding statement notes are likely to contain thoughts or concepts that pertain to a variety of different aspects of your life like how you spend your time or what you do. In the end, you won't be able to use them all. Consider who you want to reach with this remark to focus your efforts. Clients, coworkers, superiors, recruiters, publishers, and academics are all possible answers to this issue. Another possibility is a combination of targets.

3-Plan your message

Once you know who you're attempting to reach, it's time to figure out what you want to say. In a branding statement, you can communicate something personal with your audience. To make the most of this opportunity, make sure that your message is valuable and demonstrates something unique about you. For example, it could be based on your abilities, your work experience, or your views.

4-Make it unique

If you want to make an impact with your brand, you need a powerful statement. People's interpretations of this will vary. Make your message creative, insightful, educational, inspiring, or motivating. Not every scenario calls for the same approach, so be inventive.

5-Keep it short

Consider a written branding statement as your initial virtual impression before meeting someone in person. When meeting someone face-to-face, an individual's initial reaction to them is practically instinctual. Because your branding statement functions in the same way, it shouldn't be overly lengthy as well. Unless there are exceptional circumstances, try to confine your remark to one or two sentences in length.

WHEN AND HOW TO USE YOUR BRANDING STATEMENT

The appropriate branding statement can open the door to new career prospects, improved customer relationships, a broader company network, and a variety of other benefits. Create a personal brand and branding statement with the goal of communicating with your target audience in mind. Once you've created your message, you'll need to get it in front of people.

Here are seven places where you may incorporate your branding statement to ensure that your reach is as broad as possible:

RESUME: In recent years, resume formats have undergone several changes. Now a days including a personal branding statement in a goal or summary section is becoming more common. When applying for a job, it's a good idea to include a statement about your personal brand in your resume.

PERSONAL WEBPAGE: A personal webpage is an excellent approach to promote your abilities, services, experiences, and personality. This is an excellent spot to insert your branding statement.

DIGITAL OR PHYSICAL PORTFOLIO: Your portfolio, whether it's digital or physical, serves as a display for your philosophy, approach, and best work. On the first page of your portfolio, include a personal branding statement that sets the tone for the rest of the document.

PROFESSIONAL SOCIAL MEDIA ACCOUNTS: A significant amount of professional networking takes place online. Incorporating a personal branding statement into your social media platforms makes them more distinctive and attention-grabbing. Additionally, it may assist you in making connections with possible clients, employers, or other individuals of your industry who share your interests.

BUSINESS CARDS: To connect with individuals, you need to have business cards on hand. In a tiny amount of space, these cards may store a great deal of information. Incorporating a brief personal branding statement onto your business card will assist you in showcasing who you and what you have to offer.

PROFESSIONAL EMAIL: At the end of your emails, you can include a personal branding message as part of your signature. This gives your electronic messages a distinctive mark. If your branding statement is more than a phrase or two long, you should consider shortening it for this purpose.

At the office: In terms of your professional identity, your branding statement reflects who you are and what you intend to be in the future. Incorporating your personal branding statement into your professional life helps to further establish your personal brand and ideal image.

Finally, once your unique promise of value has been crafted to your satisfaction, it's time to write your personal brand statement!

Make sure to think about the main themes that come up when you write your own statement. Also, think about your strengths. Then, picture your best self!

PRACTICE WORKSHEET- MY PERSONAL BRAND STATEMENT

I AM: What are you well-known for? Please provide your job title or position here.

____

____

I HELP: Who do you provide help to in your current position?

____

____

UNDERSTAND/DO: What do you do to assist your audience, businesses, or clients in doing or understanding?

____

____

SO THAT: What kind of transformation do you want to see in your audience?

____

____

#LEAVEALEGACY

A Game Changer Elevator Pitch...!!!

An Elevator Pitch, often known as an elevator speech, is a summary of your educational and professional background. The term "Elevator Pitch" refers to the fact that it should be concise enough to be delivered during a brief elevator trip. Everything in this speech should be focused on making a strong first impression on the audience about you as a person.

Your elevator pitch is a means to convey your knowledge and credentials quickly and effectively to those who have never met you before. This short speech can help you make a strong impression on potential employers and colleagues. On your first day of work, it can help you meet new people and expand your network, as well as help you find a job and establish relationships with coworkers. The truth is that most people have given an elevator pitch even if they didn't know it. People make pitches for everything from job interviews to new business opportunities, and there are a lot of different types of pitches out there. Making sure you're ready for your next pitch is an important part of marketing both yourself and your company.

WHEN TO USE AN ELEVATOR SPEECH AND HOW TO DELIVER IT

Using your elevator pitch at job fairs and career expos, as well as online in your LinkedIn summary or Twitter bio, is a good idea if you're looking for a position. When presenting oneself to hiring managers and corporate representatives, giving an elevator speech is an excellent method to acquire confidence. If you're attending a professional association event, network gatherings or any other form of meeting, be prepared to present your elevator pitch with people you meet.

1-Your elevator speech should be short

Speeches should not exceed 30-60 seconds. You don't have to go into detail about all your previous employment and aspirations for the future. Your pitch should be a summary of who you are and what you do.

2-Persuasiveness is a must

The content of an elevator speech should be captivating enough to pique the listener's interest in your concept, organization, or background despite its brief length.

3-Bring your talents

Your elevator pitch should describe your qualifications and skills. Focus on assets that can be used in multiple contexts. This is your chance to brag a little – don't sound arrogant but do mention your talents.

4-Practice

Preparation is the key to a successful elevator speech. The more you practice it, the easier it will become. Preparation for a career networking event or job interview will help you deliver it more naturally. Keep in mind that your body language conveys as much information to the listener as your words. Practice in front of a mirror. Rehearse with a friend or videotape it. This will tell you if you're on time and presenting a coherent message. Perfect practice makes perfect. Remember that how you communicate is as essential as what you say. Without practice, you're likely to speak too quickly, sound awkward, or overlook essential pitch factors. Make it a point to practice your pitch often. The more you practice, the more natural your pitch will be. You want it to sound like a conversation, not a sales presentation.

5-Be optimistic and flexible

It's important to show that you're flexible and open-minded when delivering your pitch because you're not usually interviewing for a specific role. Always be cheerful and flexible when delivering your pitch.

6-Describe your aims

Do not go overboard with details. Since your pitch will be used by a wide range of individuals and in a wide range of situations, being overly specific isn't a great idea. But don't forget to specify what you're looking for in your message.

7-Know your audience and speak to them

Recognize who you're talking to, and tailor your message accordingly to demonstrate your understanding of the sector, utilizing jargon is an effective strategy in specific situations. However, avoid employing jargon in your elevator pitch, especially if you're talking to recruiters who may find the terminology unfamiliar and off-putting. To keep things basic, focus on a few key points.

8-Get a business card ready

Make sure you have a business card handy. To continue the conversation, if you have a business card, hand it over at the end of it. Instead, you might offer to give your contact information using your smartphone if you don't have one. If you're attending a job fair or a professional networking event, bringing a copy of your CV will help demonstrate your interest and preparedness.

9-Don't speak too quickly

Yes, you have a limited amount of time to present a great deal of information. However, do not attempt to resolve this situation by speaking rapidly. This will simply make it more difficult for your audience to comprehend your message.

10-Avoid rambling

Practicing your elevator speech is vital. While you don't want to over-rehearse and seem awkward, you also don't want to have unfocused or confusing sentences in your pitch. Give the other individual a chance to answer.

11-Avoid frowning or monotonous speech

Keep your expressions upbeat and avoid using a monotone voice. Maintain a high degree of energy, self-assurance, and enthusiasm always.

Smiling and maintaining a nice facial expression are great ways to keep people engaged in what you have to say.

12-Don't stick to one elevator pitch

Don't limit yourself to a single elevator pitch to get your message across. Perhaps you're interested in pursuing two different areas in your career.

Customize your pitch depending on who you're dealing with. Additionally, you may want to prepare a more relaxed, personal pitch for social situations.

TIPS ON HOW TO CRAFT AN ELEVATOR PITCH

In crafting an elevator pitch, it can be difficult to separate key information from irrelevant ones. That's why learning how to communicate successfully at work is crucial. Even while it's good to tailor your communications whenever feasible, it isn't required to give potential customers a comprehensive background of your company. Only the most recent and relevant information should be provided in the document. To begin crafting your own pitch, you must first grasp the essential elements of a successful elevator speech.

The introduction is the most important part of a good pitch. It could be as basic as saying your name and the company for which you work. Your elevator pitch will sound more natural if you can make it more personal. Eye contact and body language are both critical components of a strong introduction.

Here are a few pointers to bear in mind while presenting oneself to a potential prospect.

Greet your audience in a manner that is appropriate for the situation. Dress formally for a business pitch or more casually for a fun occasion. Because virtual business meetings and networking events are becoming more common, you'll need to get creative with your introductions when using video chat. You may even begin with a lighthearted joke to help break the ice. But, whatever you do, make sure it is relevant to your target audience.

Every solution begins with a problem. No matter what problem you or your company is trying to solve, it's critical that you make a strong first impression in your elevator pitch to establish a consistent tone for the rest of your presentation. For example, coordinating work amongst teams is a problem. If you can, use real-world examples to connect the problem to your audience and make it more relatable. If you do this, you might be able to make the problem more relevant to your audience and get them to pay attention. The best way to show your audience what you're talking about is to give them more than one example or a picture.

1-Provide a Solution to the Problem

If the problem is what initially captures the audience's attention, the solution is what keeps them interested. This is your opportunity to demonstrate to them why they require your assistance.

Here's an example of a possible solution: Kirti provides teams with a method for organising and managing work, allowing them to understand what they need to do, why it is important, and how to complete it.

If you want your elevator pitch to be effective, focus on the solution. For businesses, it's probable that the rapid solution pitch has already been developed and is ready to go. Then again, it's always a good idea to tailor your pitch to your audience. So don't be scared to change it to match your audience. If you're pitching to a prospective client on your own behalf, focus on the unique skills you've developed and how they'll benefit your prospect.

2-Describe your Value Proposition

You've piqued the interest of your audience; now it's time to close the deal by demonstrating why your answer is superior to everyone else's. The value proposition differs from the solution in that it focuses on why your audience should choose your solution over a competitor's. If you don't have an answer right away, conduct a competitive study to compare your offers, or go to your executive summary for guidance.

Look at your communication and interface capabilities if your market is incredibly specialized and you don't have a clear differentiation or strong competitors in your field. Consider why your idea or solution is unique enough that someone would want to put it to use in their own business.

3-Engage the Audience

Prior to concluding your presentation, it's critical to leave your audience feeling appreciated or curious about something they said or did. Never say your goodbyes in a rehearsed manner; instead, be sincere and real.

There is no one-size-fits-all strategy for enticing your audience. A genuine compliment can go a long way in closing a speech, while a question might open the door for conversation. To put an end to the conversation, go back to the reason you wanted to present your idea to them in the first place. Finally, don't forget to exchange contact information, such as a business card.

A FLAWLESS ELEVATOR PITCH TEMPLATE

Now that you know the essential components of a pitch, the next step is constructing your very own elevator pitch. This template can apply for just about every occasion, from a job interview to presenting a small business or startup.

Template for an Elevator Pitch in General

Create your speech by starting with our elevator pitch template and adding facts and personalized greetings as needed. This template integrates the four components described above to cover all of the crucial information of an effective elevator pitch.

- Introduction: "Hello, my name is [name], and I work as a [position title] at [business name]. "It's a pleasure to finally meet you!"

- Issue: "Since you work for [business name or industry], I believed you'd be interested in knowing that [problem + intriguing statistic]."

- Solution: "One of the best parts about working at [your company's name] is that we've been able to fix exactly that problem by [solution]."

- We're the only company that provides [value proposition]," says the CEO.

- Call to action (CTA): *"I believe our solution has the potential to be extremely beneficial to you. "Do you have any time this week to chat with me about this?"*

Be open to changing your pitch template to better reflect your personality and professional competence. We've also provided personalized 30-second elevator pitch examples below to serve as inspiration for personal information that you can incorporate into your speech to make it more interesting.

WORKSHEET ON CRAFTING ELEVATOR PITCH

CRAFT YOUR PITCH

Step 1- About Yourself

My Name is

____

Step 2-The strength you want to promote

Your skill, specialty, accomplishments

____

Step 3-Differentiate yourself

____

Define your Unique selling proposition (USP)

Step 4-Call to action

Be specific and tell them what you want them to do. Explain the benefits of your proposal

____

#DRESSTOIMPRESS

Power Dressing for Success…!!!

Create a strong self-branding package using visual identity principles.

The way you look determines how confident you appear to others. You'll look and feel your best when you dress according to who you are and how you like to live your life. Giving yourself the gift of self-confidence is a wonderful thing. As a result, others find you to be more relatable, fascinating, and beautiful. The correct clothing can also help you concentrate and increase your cognitive abilities.

Experts in the fields of behavior and communication agree that making a good first impression is critical in business negotiations and transactions. It has an impact on how people view you, trust you, and desire to collaborate with you. Your physical appearance is a window into your personality.

Whether or not you realize it, you have a personal brand. Even though we know there is more to a person than how he or she looks, potential clients, colleagues, and other people you encounter will make judgments based on your appearance.

It is crucial to have a professional self-presentation, or visual identity, because people create connections between what something appears to be on the outside and what it is on the inside. A long time has passed since this attitude was held.

"Wearing something makes a statement, especially in today's era of instant connections. Fashion is a form of communication" - Miuccia Prada

Choosing the right attire for each occasion necessitates careful consideration. Whether or not you turn up is the question of the day. The way you portray yourself is a visual CV of who you are and what you stand for, and it speaks volumes about your values.

Brand managers are experts in visual identity. A brand's first (and perhaps most enduring) impression is often based on how something looks. A brand's message can be quickly conveyed through product design and packaging. They provide interest and make things more memorable. They may even be able to close the deal.

Color, shape, and material are all ways that a brand's packaging and design communicate with us. Brands use images and symbols in their logos, packaging, and advertising to tell people what they are about and how they can help them. The same is true of people. Each aspect of one's personality is conveyed through their appearance—from their shoes to the watch they wear, their haircut to their grin (or frown). People build their impressions of you based on what they see and hear from you.

STEPS FOR DRESSING FOR YOUR PERSONAL BRANDING

1-TAKE ADVANTAGE OF THE FIRST TWO SECONDS

In a couple of seconds, we are labelled as excellent or awful, hire able Unhireable, hip or stodgy, successful, or unsuccessful, likeable, or dislikeable. In the first few seconds, everything happens. It's a place we've all been. The job candidate hasn't even walked through the door yet and has already been assessed. Perhaps we've even excluded that individual from consideration. Snap visual impressions are used to make the decision, such as how people enter the room, how they appear, their clothing, how they present themselves, their facial expressions, and their body language. Even though they haven't said anything, we have formed opinions about who they are and what they are like

Our first impression will be etched in our minds forever. There are times when we make quick judgements based on how someone looks, but everyone does it. We're wired to be more attracted to people who are attractive. People who have good looks are consistently regarded as brighter, more personable, intelligent, successful, and superior in a variety of other aspects of their lives. With the right marketing strategy, "interesting" looks can be effective branding tools.

2-IDENTIFY YOUR PERSONAL STYLE

To begin, you must ascertain your own identity. Consider the words that best express your personal values and who you are. Develop a personal sense of style and appearance that reflects your personality. Become more confident in your style and appearance by establishing a personal identity. It's important to have a distinct style that people will remember about you when they see your face. Be aware that just because something is lovely, it does not guarantee that it will fit or be in fashion with you. Invest the necessary time and effort into developing your personal style and discovering what looks nice on you.

Your wardrobe can convey a range of emotions, aspirations, spending patterns and conscious consumption

3-DISCOVER THE MAGIC WITHIN YOU

Self-branding is a skill that no one can learn overnight. We must start with our identity and appearance. Our identity is rooted in our physical appearance. This is true regardless of how great or weak your visual identity is. Everything, however, could grow. Brands often languish until someone with the right mix of intelligence and imagination comes along to resurrect and maximize their value. To begin, you must focus on your own well-being. Don't start by mimicking the looks of those you adore. It's nice to be inspired, but if you're just a clone of someone else, you won't be recognized. Your visual identity should reflect who you are and what you like. You should choose a visual identity that reflects your personality and aesthetic preferences. The creation of a personal visual inventory is a fantastic method to get started on building your visual identity. What is your most distinguishing characteristic? What is the most annoying feature? Find out what makes you unique and what makes you happy (height, shape, hair, features, expressions). What should you put the most emphasis on? What should you stress? Or underline?

4-WHAT DOES YOUR VISUAL IDENTITY SAY ABOUT YOU?

Your visual identity tells the world a lot about who you are. Creating a visual identity is all about conveying the message you're trying to get across. When it all comes together, the visual identity and the message are one and the same. Look at your appearance and the clothes you wear. What impression do you want to leave on the world? If so, is it in keeping with your overall brand identity It's possible to enhance your visual identity by using a distinctive feature or trademark item. If you want to get the most out of your visual identity, you need to address all these issues. Ineffectiveness occurs when you don't communicate the appropriate message

5-CREATE VISUAL JOY

Visually excite the audience. Your brand's worth is substantially accelerated if it has an engaging visual identity. The Godfather, Part III was the first film in which Sofia Coppola came into the public eye and was widely disliked. Actor to independent director was a game changer for her self-image. It's no wonder Marc Jacobs chose her as his model because of her unique look and cool personality.

Tennis superstars like Venus Williams, Serena Williams, and Andre Agassi have a fantastic sense of style and a cool image, but it is unlikely that this has helped them win more matches. However, they were instrumental in assisting these sportsmen in developing strong brand identities that resulted in higher-paying endorsement contracts.

WHAT DOES IT MEAN TO DRESS FOR SUCCESS?

If you want to present yourself in a professional manner at work, you must dress in business attire and accessories appropriately. Dressing for work requires modesty, well-tailored tailoring, and a lack of any sort of graphic or image. Your clothing should be free of rips, holes, and stains, and should be freshly laundered. For example, while a suit may be required in one workplace, khaki slacks and an official polo shirt are acceptable attire at another, depending on the workplace's level of formality. Learn about your company's specific policies by consulting the manual you received when you joined.

A good initial impression

The way you look can be the first thing people notice about you. When you meet new individuals at work, you want to make a good first impression. This is especially vital during interviews and for meeting senior managers who are responsible for recruiting and promotion. Your long-term reputation might be shaped by the first impressions others have of you.

To convey your professionalism

It's important to present yourself in a professional manner if you want to be taken seriously at work. It displays that you care about how you look and put effort into maintaining a professional image at work. When you show others that you take your job seriously, they are more likely to regard and see you as a valuable resource.

To represent your firm

As a member of your organization, you represent the company to the public. In any setting, the way you present yourself has an impact on the company you're representing. Make sure your organization's image is conveyed in a positive light by dressing professionally. Trying to look well-groomed and put-together will enhance your impression, regardless of whether you're wearing business casual or a uniform. For employers, it's a good sign when employees see themselves as public face of the company.

For self-assurance

You can accomplish your finest work when you are at your best. Professional attire may help you feel motivated and confident to take on new tasks, meet new people, and advance in your job. While other aspects of your work life may be out of your hands, how you present yourself is something you can control and use. Your image is your own brand. It often tells people who don't know you a lot about you. Dress professionally to reflect your ambitions, personality, and creativity.

Make you feel part of the team

Many professional contexts require the ability to collaborate with others to be successful. A well-dressed appearance gives you the confidence to interact with colleagues and superiors, as well as the sense that you have something meaningful to say and contribute. If you present yourself as professional and dedicated, your coworkers are more likely to include you in crucial talks and projects.

Boost your credibility

People respond positively to professionalism, often interacting more and trusting what you say. Professional attire may enhance your reputation with coworkers, bosses, clients, and the public.

#HUMANBRAND

Inspire and Influence...!!!

Your personal brand has the potential to open doors and facilitate the development of long-term relationships and career prospects. The people you interact with and the way your brand is regarded by others will have a major impact on the network you're aiming to build. It has the potential to reach future supervisors and team members. Additionally, it is applicable to both online and off-line mediums.

There are various Social Networks where you can brand yourself. You can be selective about those social networks if you have limited time and resources too.

We may start with Podcast, which is an innovative way of branding your image.

Dr Pooja says,

'Podcasting, as a media, is not a new phenomenon. However, it has been on a steady ascent for several years now and continues to do so massively. It's safe to say that podcasting has hit a tipping point in terms of popularity.

This isn't a surprise, either. Because of its inexpensive production costs and ease of use, podcasting has emerged as the preferred method of reaching niche audiences. These traits have made the medium ideal for anyone who want to develop a strong personal brand. If you're a podcaster, you'll face the difficulty of creating a show that not only stands apart from the rest of your peers, but also demonstrates your own personal brand. Choosing the right format for your brand's narrative will help you convey it in the most effective way possible for you and your audience.'

Some of your options are as follows:

Solo talking head: There is only one talking head. You will be the only one who will be speaking various issues that you believe will be of interest to your audience. Current events, tutorials, opinions, and other useful information or subjects can be covered on your show.

Interview style: In the style of an interview in addition to adding an exciting element to your presentation, this format may also provide you with the ability to harness influencers to assist you in increasing the number of followers on your page.

Narrative style: Style is narrative in nature. This type of podcast is story-driven, and it will require a large amount of editing to make it a cohesive plot.

Multi-hosting: If you choose this arrangement, you will be co-hosting the show with one or more other people. This is particularly useful if you want your listeners to hear more than one point of view or piece of feedback on the topic at hand.

Participate as a guest on other podcasts

It may do wonders for your brand to get interviewed on top podcasts in your niche, especially if the podcasts are well-known. You must, however, first get on the radar of those top podcasters and provide them with a compelling reason to invite you to their shows. While this may appear to be difficult, it is fairly simple if you know what you're doing.

The Process of Developing Your Own Show

With little doubt, having your own podcast is a powerful experience—not only do you have the freedom to host your own show, but you also have the ability to customise your content in any way you like. As if that weren't enough, podcasting isn't all that difficult or expensive to do.

Tips for Using Podcasting to Promote Your Business or Brand

1. Get the ball rolling: It is not enough to simply sit back and watch your competitors grow their audiences through excellent podcast content while you twiddle your thumbs wondering 'what if.' When you finally get started, be certain that the audio you generate is of excellent quality and has a clean tone.

2. Be one-of-a-kind. Every successful brand has its own distinctive voice. Check out these podcasts to have a better understanding of what I'm talking about! Consider the brands you admire – what distinguishes them from the competition? There must be a compelling reason for consumers to choose to listen to your podcast above other similar programmes. It will come down to whether people enjoy your personality, the themes you address, and the way you deliver them. Don't be afraid to express yourself.

3. Consider your target audience: What exactly do they want to hear from you about? Think about what subjects they would like you to cover because you are creating the podcast for them (not for yourself!) and not for yourself. As a starting point, consider past queries you've been asked or the most typical challenges your company is now experiencing as a starting point. The rest will just happen on its own accord.

4. Maintain consistency: Maintain the schedule you established – weekly, biweekly, or monthly – because people will want to know, for example, that every Tuesday, yoursite.com has a fantastic new audio session available for them to listen and enjoy.

5. Display visually appealing artwork: To develop brand recognition, professional-looking artwork is essential, and this is no different when it comes to building your business through podcasting. When utilizing iTunes, the suggested specifications for the artwork that will be embedded on your RSS Feed are 300 × 300 pixels in either the JPG or PNG format, with a resolution of 300 pixels. Maintain consistency in your image across all your online brand's outlets. This makes it simple for people to recognize you in search results - a wonderful example of this is the artwork for my podcast.

6. Include tags in your iTunes submissions and set up an RSS feed for your contributions: This will make it easier for people to find your podcast in the iTunes store, resulting in more casual passersby becoming subscribers and, ultimately, fans.

7. Contact other podcasters: Even while it may appear that you are putting yourself in bed with your competition, you really need to get as involved with your 'competition' as possible. As with mastermind groups, listening to their podcasts offers you with the opportunity to learn from them, hear what they are saying, and, as with mastermind groups, you may even get some amazing ideas from them.

8. Promote your podcast: To accomplish this, you must submit your channel and RSS Feed to podcast directories not only in the iTunes store, but also in other sites like as the Zune Marketplace, Blackberry Podcast, Miro Guide, Stitcher, DoubleTwist, and Blubrry. This is a new one for me, and I've already been featured on Stitcher — the rest of the episodes are now in the works.

9. Use your imagination: Numerous firms and entrepreneurs are already experimenting with podcasting; therefore, your content must be standout, engaging, and full of original ideas. In this case, everything from the introduction in your podcast to your associated brand artwork, website design, and the use of social media will be considered. Make an impression.

10. Don't forget to advertise your other platforms: In your podcast, take advantage of the opportunity to mention your Facebook and Twitter pages, as well as your blog or corporate website at some point in the conversation. This provides you with more opportunities to contact your audience and, in turn, produce more subscriptions, listeners, and income, as well as expand your audience through viral sharing. Keep in mind that if you overindulge, it will become 'out of date' very quickly.

11. Add value and make yourself memorable: Overall, this should be always your number one priority. It will ensure that your brand will develop because of podcasting. Customers will keep coming back and downloading your podcast – as well as sharing it with their friends – if you establish yourself as a thought leader in your profession, a go-to person, or an authority (whatever you choose to name yourself!).

Let us now speak of blogging where bloggers started writing for a close-knit set of people. Writing for a few friends and followers became a trend initially. Not many people were eager to go and read the blogs and also their fresh perspectives were not welcoming. But if you observe these days, blogging has become a huge trend. There is a lot of space for new and fresh opinions, and they are warmly welcomed. Readers are interested in understanding different angles of the same issues and appreciate them on the social platform. People across are passionate about many things. It could include photography, food, fitness, make-up, motherhood and lot many other things.

In the early days, women followed a muted theory, i.e., their voice was suppressed, and they did not have a choice but to stay quiet about their opinions. Gone are those days! But now, women are inclined towards blogging because it is convenient for them to raise their opinions and show their voice to the public. Also, people are interested in reading about what matters to them the most.

People are interested in creating communities where people of similar interest come together to share information via blogs, and also speak of upcoming other topics.

Setting up a blog is easy. There are lot of different platforms where you can start writing and have maximum visibility to the information shared. You may choose a template for your blog. It is interesting to have different fonts and colors on the piece of write up that you would like to share with the readers. The game changer could be choosing an easy URL. You may want to tell you circle of influence about your blog and hence you may want to promote it without any difficulty. You may be sure of no special characters, any abbreviations, and incorrect spellings. Also, the pronunciation should be easy so that your circle of influence remembers your blog URL for life!

You may choose a template according to the content you want to share. Template could be a little fun with pop colors or a professional looking one. The template should be easy to modify and customize. You will be spoilt for choice when it comes to choosing a template. Choose wisely! Different platforms have different options of templates to start with. Platforms like Wordpress.org offer the maximum choice of platforms. It is always a great idea to not keep changing the templates very often. Consistency could be the key to readers following your blogs and having the maximum engagement with them.

It is greatly important to find your expertise of writing. Your blog cannot have all the information under the sky. A specific set of readers will be attracted towards your blog. Hence, targeting the right audience and keeping in mind our own interest is of prime importance. This way you may certainly become a subject matter expert and establish your expertise in a specific field. It also helps the readers to relate and engage with your posts. Thus, your piece of information may get highlighted and connect you to other established bloggers in your field. It is called a community building!

Finding your niche may be easy and difficult at the same time. Understanding what drives you towards the topic is important. The more you are interested in writing about a certain topic, the more often you will write. This helps in establishing consistency of writing and posting your blogs. Writing once a week is ideal for the bloggers to construct a write up and also for the readers to engage with the post. They may find it worth commenting and you as a blogger must reply to their messages and respect their perspectives on your topic. You may create your own blogging schedule. This will certainly help to build your own positive personal brand with respect to writing fresh pieces. You also have the liberty to choose the length of the blog. You may analyze your readers capacity on certain topics and the length may vary accordingly.

LinkedIn

LinkedIn brings you an unique opportunity to connect with people all around the globe and help your personal brand reach higher heights. The platform has more than 90 million users which makes the platform valuable and helps you build connections with ex employers, current employers, and future connections.

The most important part of building your personal brand on LinkedIn is creating and writing about yourself. Adding people, you know and showing maximum connections is another game changer. You may like to showcase your work and your presence in the industry. Highlighting your education and area of expertise helps people to connect with you. Remember, this is your professional brand but overlapping personal and professional brand is also important. You can have two images and two different brands for the same person. Maintaining consistency in your brand professionally and personally will help others to establish an easy connect with you. Your profile photo will also do a lot of talking about you and your image. Professional photograph usually works well with LinkedIn. Connections certainly appreciate your professional approach on LinkedIn. It is also an intelligent move to use the same picture on every platform to maintain your brand consistency.

Recommending your friends will also be valuable to them and you as well. Recommendations play well with your work expertise and how are you as a person to work with. It is also fairly important to build connections with your trusted contacts. This will take you miles ahead in terms of recommendations and commenting on your posts for better. This will certainly make the LinkedIn experience surreal and have better involvement with the people you know.

There is great power in staying in touch with your connections. People all over the globe would like to be professionally active rather than on being available on Instagram or Facebook for fun. LinkedIn is a community of white-collar professionals who appreciate establishing connections with other professionals in the same industry or across. These connections may certainly add credibility to your professional brand. You may not like asking for recommendations. But if you write one for someone in your connections, you may certainly receive one. This may help is maintaining great relationships and engaging with your connections.

Twitter

Imaging yourself on a platform where million users are actively tweeting on daily basis and share their opinions on latest trends. Engaging yourself in latest conversations may help you getting followers and inspire people around the globe. Sharing your perspectives on a topic that's important to you may help you find like minded people and create a community for yourself. Imagine around 800 tweets per second and the way the platform is growing into billions of users. Your tweet may not be read by everyone, but certainly by some set of people who are interested in the same topic as yours. This has changed the way of communication for people and help them set up a group of people who can bring a change in the society by raising their voices. Masses may perceive your personal brand in a specific way related to the information you are sharing.

For this platform too, establishing your expertise is of prime importance. The platform has lot to offer but you should be able to share your story and help people to share your story on their walls. This is an unique opportunity to talk about different issues with billions of users. This platform is growing exponentially and helping the users to make friends and establish stronger associations. You may not have thousands of followers, but you may have a specific set of readers who connect with you regularly. These readers may further re tweet or share your content which may help in strengthening your brand. Re tweeting is a trend to create longer conversations on the topic which may need attention. It is a great way to reach out to people and make them aware of what's happening. Hence, tweeting for the readers and being yourself may help in growing your brand.

Sometimes just writing a quote or penning down some random thoughts also is a refreshing wave of breeze to the readers. They may be already bored of the content that's on the platform, and you may like to bring in some motivation or enthusiasm to your readers. It is not always essential to speak of topics which are important and need to be addressed. It may also be a small push factor for Monday Blues. You really don't know, who needs it today! Make your followers smile an laugh with your witty one liners on some days to gain attention and yet be genuine.

Make a point to be your self and not fake a personality which is unknown to you. Personal branding relates and is built on the facts of how you are and how real you can be. Being unfiltered and unapologetically true is what will help you sustain your personal brand in the long run.

#LIVEYOURBRAND

Substantiate Yourself...!!

There could never be any other brand which could be more attractive than 'OURSELVES'. Your values, personality, culture, and the amalgamation of all these makes you a brand, it helps you to substantiate yourself. Now, why Live your Brand? Is it essential, necessary and that important? The answer is Yes. Because you can't pretend to be someone else and grow your brand. You need to understand yourself and help the pieces fit completely. Your actions will reflect your values and the integrity. Hence, people around you have a clear understanding of you as a person and do not carry a blurred image of you. This helps in not only being transparent but also build a stronger relationship with others. Figuring out who you are, will certainly have high positive effect on your relationship with yourself. And to do all this, you don't have to always 'Stand Out', you can very well 'Blend In' and still be relevant, distinctive and consistent.

Courage is another important factor which each person has, but in different ways. But surely, in personal branding, consistency takes a lot of courage. Consistency leads to firm beliefs, positive impression of how you are on people's mind. Your life experiences help you lot to create good impression.

This book presents to you the mantra to #LiveYourBrand. The 5 C's will help you differentiate yourself and at the same time differentiate yourself in the crowd.

1. Content – Content you bring to the world is the most important part to live your brand. Stronger the content, stronger your values, and stronger your brand.

2. Character – Your character will be a mirror to the world. Reflecting what you are will take you miles ahead in the process of personal branding.

3. Clarity – Clarity of what you are, who you are and presenting the same to everyone plays a key role in living your brand each day.

4. Credibility – How credible you are as a person and how much people around you can rely on you can be your key differentiator.

5. Consistency – People love the polar star, fixed and bright all the time. The more you disappear, people will lose the connect with you. Consistency in digital or physical world will help you be more relevant and make you more reliable.

Living your brand each could be difficult but meeting more and more people will bring lot of varied experiences to share. Easier said than done. The truth is not everyone who meets you will like you as you are. They would expect a lot of great things from you. But remember, not to please everyone by changing ourselves. There could be lots of things which help in reputation building. Spending time with oneself brings a lot of understanding to improve ourselves as a person. It also helps in making greater contributions to the society which may bring in immense respect and make ourselves proud. Different people may have different perceptions of you, which may kill your positivity or playful vibe. But at the same time, it is important to not let these people change your 5 C's. In this whole process, it is very easy to change ourselves as a person and wear a mask of an influencer. Emotions may override your personality in such cases. Be sure to maintain your moral and have high regard for the people who made you realize what hate could be. It would surely be killing their vibe with kindness. This incredible and long-lasting relationship with oneself will lead to consistent reputation to stay intact in the society.

Dr Priyanka's experience:

'I am glad to have a great experience when it comes to Personal Branding. 90% of the people I know in my family and friends around me can resonate with me well. My work has a great reflection on the society and has been

pitched well to different parts of the society. I have been incredibly grateful for the overwhelming response by my students, colleagues, and friends.

I have been in academics where I could inspire and not just influence people around me. The case studies written on my personal failures and success have been a huge hit amongst the public. They resonate with my personality and my reputation. My website too is a word of my actions which unexpectedly grew in many directions.

My social media account and my research area have also been the same which helped me to contribute to the field of influencer marketing. My body of work says what kind of person am I. It shows how communicative and reliable my work ethic has been.

With the mantra of live your brand, I could certainly shift to industry and showcase my expertise in various field of technology. I could fairly impress people with my stories and be relevant with the world.'

But having said all this, in the process of being distinctive, some people may lose out on themselves. One needs to understand that being relevant helps your desire grow. This make bring in a differentiator in you. But that may not be appreciated by all. You can't be relevant to all, or serve the needs of all parts of the society. One needs to target the market well and see for yourself what part of you could be more relevant to them. You should not try to be the most relevant person in the room, but you can be the most honest and appealing in the room. Let's be more acknowledged and recognize who we are and be unapologetic for the person we are. One must remember personal branding is not a compromise done on who you really are and your core values.

You and us have been on an incredible and inseparable journey of personal branding through this book. We have tried to put together some most important tactics of personal branding. We thank all the readers for being open to new theories and new possibilities in personal branding. We are sure to have brought some great and impeccable skills in personal branding that would help you blend in yet stand out. We have tried to cover the positioning to brand strategy and some digital marketing aspects as well. This era requires you to be hands on technology and impress people digitally too. Your digital avatar is a credible and critical brand to analyze.

This book will help every person their whole life who want to create an impactful difference by being yourself. It will also help you explore new areas to build and enhance your brand periodically.

We have kept different audiences in our minds who require personal branding in their life or career. We have tried to build an eco-system of branding to inspire and not just influence. You may also feel so many concepts put together at first and difficult to choose one, but we bet you a good personal brand if you know yourself well and use the right technique to showcase it. This book and your actions goals together will certainly help any individual to achieve the greatest heights and overcome personal branding challenges.

We hope you an empowered brand of yourselves!!!